D1518475

THE
NATIONAL MALL

BY JAMIE KALLIO

CONTENT CONSULTANT
Dr. Lisa Benton-Short
Professor of Geography
George Washington University

Cover image: There are many iconic landmarks on the National Mall.

Core Library

An Imprint of Abdo Publishing
abdobooks.com

abdobooks.com

Published by Abdo Publishing, a division of ABDO, PO Box 398166, Minneapolis, Minnesota 55439. Copyright © 2020 by Abdo Consulting Group, Inc. International copyrights reserved in all countries. No part of this book may be reproduced in any form without written permission from the publisher. Core Library™ is a trademark and logo of Abdo Publishing.

Printed in the United States of America, North Mankato, Minnesota
092019
012020

THIS BOOK CONTAINS
RECYCLED MATERIALS

Cover Photo: Shutterstock Images
Interior Photo: Shutterstock Images, 1, 4–5, 30; iStockphoto, 7; Tinnaporn Sathapornnanont/ Shutterstock Images, 8, 43; North Wind Picture Archives, 10–11, 12, 15; Charles R. Parsons/Currier & Ives/Library of Congress, 16–17; Travel View/Shutterstock Images, 20–21; National Capital Planning Commission, Washington, DC/Wikimedia Commons, 23; World History Archive/Newscom, 25; Dick Swanson/The LIFE Images Collection/Getty Images, 28–29; Orhan Cam/Shutterstock Images, 33, 38 (bottom right); Sean Pavone/Shutterstock Images, 36–37; Douglas Litchfield/ Shutterstock Images, 38 (top right); Zak Zeinert/Shutterstock Images, 38 (top left); Luna Marina/ Shutterstock Images, 38 (bottom left); TJ Brown/Shutterstock Images, 45

Editor: Maddie Spalding
Series Designer: Claire Vanden Branden

Library of Congress Control Number: 2019905517

Publisher's Cataloging-in-Publication Data

Names: Kallio, Jamie, author.
Title: The national mall / by Jamie Kallio
Description: Minneapolis, Minnesota : Abdo Publishing, 2020 | Series: Iconic America | Includes online resources and index.
Identifiers: ISBN 9781532190919 (lib. bdg.) | ISBN 9781532176760 (ebook)
Subjects: LCSH: National Mall (Washington, D.C.)--Juvenile literature. | Washington (D.C.) --Buildings, structures, etc--Juvenile literature. | United States Capitol (Washington, D.C.)--Juvenile literature. | Monuments--Washington (D.C.)--Juvenile literature. | Washington (D.C.)--History--Juvenile literature.
Classification: DDC 917.530--dc23

CONTENTS

AMERICA'S FRONT YARD

Mariana's ride on the Smithsonian Carousel ended. She climbed off her colorful horse and joined her family. They were touring the National Mall in Washington, DC. The National Mall is an area with monuments, memorials, and parks. It also has many museums. The cheerful carousel in the middle of the National Mall was a surprise.

After lunch, Mariana and her family would visit the Smithsonian National Air and Space Museum. Mariana wanted to ride a flight simulator. The simulator shows people what it is like to fly a plane.

The Smithsonian Carousel opened in 1967.

5

Tomorrow, Mariana and her family planned to visit the Smithsonian National Museum of Natural History. Her brother wanted to see Henry. Henry is a large African elephant on display at the museum. Later, Mariana and her family would visit the Smithsonian National Museum of American History. There was just so much to do at the National Mall.

PERSPECTIVES

THE NATIONAL AIR AND SPACE MUSEUM

The National Air and Space Museum is the most-visited museum in the country. More than 7 million people visit the museum each year. Linda St. Thomas is the chief spokesperson for the Smithsonian Institution. She thinks the free admission is part of what makes the National Air and Space Museum so popular. But the main attraction is the museum's vast collection of aircraft and spacecraft.

WITHIN THE RECTANGLE

The National Mall is often called "America's Front Yard." It is part of the National Mall and Memorial Parks. This is the most-visited US national park.

THE NATIONAL MALL TODAY

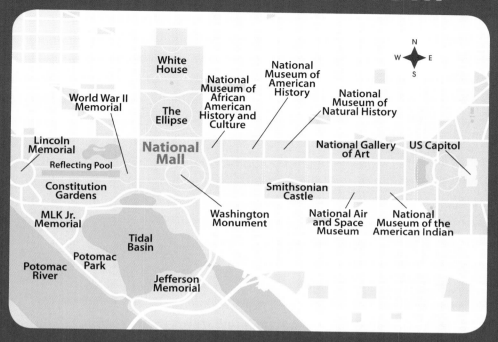

This map of the National Mall (the green space) shows where some museums and other landmarks are located. How is the National Mall organized? Why do you think it is organized this way?

More than 25 million people visit it each year. National parks are areas set aside by the federal government as places of natural or cultural importance.

The Lincoln Memorial is on the west end of the National Mall by the Potomac River. The US Capitol is on the east end. The US Congress meets in the Capitol.

The National Mall is approximately 2 miles (3 km) long.

The White House is on the north side of the National Mall. The US president lives and works in the White House. A memorial to former president Thomas Jefferson sits on the National Mall's south side. Constitution Avenue borders the National Mall on the north side. Independence Avenue is on the south side. Inside the rectangle are many monuments, memorials, and museums. Visitors will also find galleries and gardens.

SITES AND ATTRACTIONS

The National Mall and Memorial Parks contain more than 160 monuments and memorials. Some of the most popular sites are the Washington Monument and the Lincoln Memorial. The Washington Monument honors President George Washington. It is a tall marble obelisk. The Lincoln Memorial honors President Abraham Lincoln. It is a marble statue of Lincoln inside a temple. These are just a few of the many attractions that draw people to the National Mall.

THE WASHINGTON MONUMENT

Architect Robert Mills designed the Washington Monument. Construction of the monument began in 1848. The Washington National Monument Society funded the project. It later ran out of money. Congress was reluctant to pay for the monument. Construction was interrupted during the American Civil War (1861–1865). Due to these obstacles, the monument was not completed until 1885. It became the world's tallest building after its completion. Today, visitors can reach the observation deck by elevator or by climbing 897 steps.

CHAPTER
TWO

THE MALL'S EARLY HISTORY

Washington, DC, has not always been the US capital. The United States was formed in 1776. Northern cities such as New York City served as temporary capitals. But Southern lawmakers did not want the capital to be so far north. Congress members met from 1789 to 1791 to discuss a new location. They struck a deal. The new capital would be more centrally located.

On July 16, 1790, President George Washington signed the Residence Act. This act gave him the power to pick a permanent site

The capital city was surrounded on three sides by waterways.

11

George Washington, *middle*, became the first US president on April 30, 1789.

for the capital city. He chose the site for the capital in 1791. The site was in Maryland and Virginia along the Potomac and Anacostia Rivers. The capital was originally 100 square miles (260 sq km) in size. Washington called it the "Federal City."

A SYMBOL OF DEMOCRACY

The United States was a young country. Leaders had established a democracy. In a democracy, leaders listen to the country's citizens. The public has a say in how the country is governed. This was different from the types of government in most European countries. US government leaders wanted to prove to the rest of the world that a democracy could be effective. They wanted to create an impressive capital city.

In March 1791, Washington hired engineer Pierre L'Enfant to design the city. L'Enfant imagined a wide area he called the "Grand Avenue." The Grand Avenue would be lined with trees. It would connect important sites throughout the city, including monuments and fountains. This area would later be called the National Mall.

In September 1791, leaders met to decide what to call the capital and the surrounding district. They decided to call the district the "Territory of Columbia." The district contained the capital as well as two other cities: Georgetown and Alexandria. Alexandria had been taken from Virginia. The leaders changed the

A UNIQUE CITY

Government leaders wanted the US capital city to be different from major cities in other parts of the world. Major European cities such as Paris, France, did not have neat and orderly streets. Leaders wanted the capital's streets to be laid out neatly. L'Enfant wanted the capital to be open and welcoming to all people. This was meant to symbolize a democracy. L'Enfant left room at street crossings to build monuments.

capital's name to the "City of Washington." They chose this name to honor the president. The City of Washington officially became the permanent capital on December 1, 1800.

CONSTRUCTION CHALLENGES

The White House and the Capitol were some of the first buildings constructed in the new city. Then the War of 1812 (1812–1815) began. The War of 1812 was a conflict between the United States and Great Britain. In 1814, British troops invaded the City of Washington. They set fire to the White House and the Capitol.

The British army burned down the White House in 1814. It took approximately three years to rebuild the White House.

Shortly after this attack, the United States and Great Britain signed a treaty. The treaty ended the war.

In 1846, Virginia officials decided to take back Alexandria. The Territory of Columbia shrank in size. It lost one-third of its total area.

By 1850, the grounds of the National Mall were still undeveloped. There were few trees and no gardens. Millard Fillmore was the US president at the time. He hired landscaper Andrew Downing. Downing wanted the National Mall to be a park. He saw it as a living

This image shows what the capital city looked like in the late 1800s.

museum of trees and shrubs. He planned to create six parks on the National Mall. But Congress did not give him enough funding to accomplish all of his plans. He died in 1852 before he could complete his vision of the National Mall.

THE CIVIL WAR

In the mid-1800s, tensions between northern and southern states were high. Many northerners opposed slavery. Southern states relied on slavery.

Eleven southern states seceded between 1860 and 1861. They became the Confederate States of America, or the Confederacy. Northern states made up the Union. In 1861, war broke out between the Union and the Confederacy. This conflict became known as the American Civil War (1861–1865).

The Union army set up headquarters near the White House. The Confederate capital was in nearby Richmond, Virginia. Union troops helped defend the

PERSPECTIVES

SLAVERY IN THE CAPITAL

Before the Civil War, the Territory of Columbia relied on slavery. The territory was created from parts of Virginia and Maryland, which were slaveholding states. It became a center for slave trade. Slave dealers kept enslaved people in crowded pens and prisons. Enslaved people helped build the White House and other government buildings. Clarence Lusane is an African American author and historian. He said, "They [enslaved people] were building the city as a whole. It took ten years, and you can be pretty sure that given the work—and the possibility of injuries, diseases, and accidents—that people died." Slavery was finally outlawed in the territory in 1862.

Territory of Columbia in case of an attack.

The Union won the war in 1865. Then the Confederate states rejoined the Union. After the war, the City of Washington's population grew so much that it expanded beyond the city's original boundaries. The Territory of Columbia was renamed in 1871. It became the District of Columbia. The capital became known as Washington, DC.

STRAIGHT TO THE
SOURCE

Francis Baily was an English astronomer. He visited the City of Washington in 1796. He wrote:

> The view from here is extremely delightful: On each side, a fine river, flowing with a gentle current along the base of a hilly and romantic country. . . . In the rear is the still nearer view of Georgetown, and of the president's House and the Capitol. All tend to render it one of the most delightful and pleasant sites for a town I have ever remarked in the whole of the United States.

Source: Francis Baily. "Our White House: Looking In, Looking Out." *The National Children's Book and Literacy Alliance*. The National Children's Book and Literacy Alliance, n.d. Web. Accessed May 24, 2019.

Consider Your Audience

Adapt this passage for a different audience, such as your friends. Write a blog post conveying this same information for the new audience. How does your post differ from the original text and why?

EXPANSION AND CIVIL RIGHTS

Many parts of the country had to be rebuilt after the Civil War. Construction of the National Mall continued slowly. By the early 1900s, the National Mall still did not look like how L'Enfant had imagined it. Railroad tracks had been built to bring people and goods into the capital city. But they were not incorporated well into the National Mall. They crossed over the area and were out of place. Many of the city's residents disliked the tracks.

The Smithsonian Castle, which contains the Smithsonian Visitor Center, was one of the first buildings on the National Mall.

Architects again focused on developing the city and the National Mall. In 1902, Senator James McMillan started a committee called the Senate Park Commission. The commission included famous architects such as Daniel Burnham. They put together a report on how to improve the city and its parks. The report was called the McMillan Plan.

THE MCMILLAN PLAN

The McMillan Plan followed some of L'Enfant's original designs. L'Enfant's designs had included wide avenues, public squares, and elaborate buildings. The new plan called for major changes. The railroad tracks were removed. The National Mall was expanded west.

As part of the plan, L'Enfant's Grand Avenue was relandscaped. Rows of American elm trees were planted around the lawn. This area became the center of the National Mall.

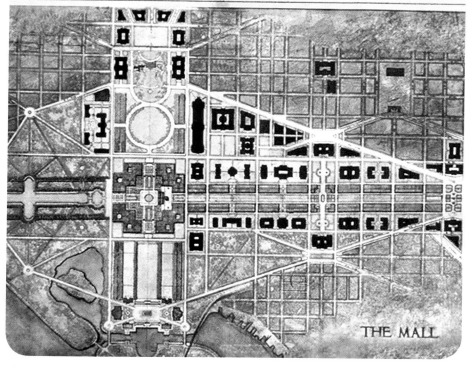

THE McMILLAN PLAN : 1901 - THE MALL

THE MALL

The McMillan Plan mapped out the committee's vision for the National Mall.

FAMOUS MEMORIALS

New sites were added to the National Mall over the next few decades. Construction on the Lincoln Memorial began in 1915. The memorial was finished in 1922. Architect Henry Bacon designed it.

PERSPECTIVES

MARIAN ANDERSON'S PERFORMANCE

In 1939, Howard University invited African American singer Marian Anderson to perform in Washington, DC. Organizers initially planned for her to sing in Constitution Hall. The Daughters of the American Revolution (DAR) owned the hall. The DAR did not want Anderson to sing there because she was African American. Anderson's performance was moved outdoors to the Lincoln Memorial. Approximately 75,000 people attended the event. Kosti Vehanen accompanied Anderson on the piano. He later remembered that Anderson's voice was "filled with deep, tragic feeling, as though the sound came from under the earth."

More memorials were later built to honor other historic figures. The Ulysses S. Grant Memorial opened in 1922. It honors Union general and US president Ulysses S. Grant. The Jefferson Memorial opened in 1943.

THE CIVIL RIGHTS MOVEMENT

While the National Mall expanded in the early and mid-1900s, the American civil rights movement was going on. This movement's

Singer Marian Anderson's historic 1939 performance on the National Mall was recorded and shared through a radio broadcast.

goal was to help African Americans gain equal rights.

Civil rights activists wanted to end racial segregation.

Racial segregation laws were one form of discrimination.

These laws separated black people from white people.

Black people had to use separate services and facilities,

THE LONGEST WALK

In the summer of 1978, the American Indian Movement (AIM) organized a march. AIM is a group that advocates for Native Americans' civil rights. The US government was trying to restrict Native people's land and water rights. Approximately 2,000 people participated in AIM's march to bring attention to this issue. They walked from San Francisco, California, to the National Mall. This journey took five months. It was called the Longest Walk.

such as schools and bathrooms. These services and facilities were often much worse than those provided to white people.

THE MARCH ON WASHINGTON

On August 28, 1963, a major civil rights protest took place on the National Mall. More than 200,000 people gathered around the Lincoln Memorial. They were taking part in the March on Washington for Jobs and Freedom. Activists protested discrimination and segregation. The march had begun at the Washington Monument. It ended at the Lincoln Memorial. Civil rights leaders gave speeches in front of the memorial. Martin Luther King Jr. gave his famous "I Have a Dream" speech. He spoke about a future without racial violence or hatred.

The march encouraged government officials to pass civil rights laws. The Civil Rights Act of 1964 ended segregation. It also banned employment discrimination based on race and other factors. The Voting Rights Act of 1965 banned obstacles that kept black people from voting.

EXPLORE ONLINE

Chapter Three explores the history of the National Mall in the 1900s. The video at the website below goes into more depth on this topic. As you know, every source is different. What information does the website give about this history? How is the information from the website the same as the information in Chapter Three? What new information did you learn?

THE NATIONAL MALL
abdocorelibrary.com/national-mall

PROTESTS AND CHANGES

In the mid- to late 1900s, the National Mall played a role in many social movements. Because it was a symbol of democracy, the National Mall was a place where many people went to protest government actions.

In the 1960s, the United States was involved in the Vietnam War (1954–1975). The war was a conflict between North and South Vietnam. A Communist government controlled North Vietnam. It wanted to control South Vietnam too. The United States allied with South Vietnam. It did not want Communism to spread.

In 1967, activists gathered near the Lincoln Memorial to protest the Vietnam War.

Today, the US troops who died in the Vietnam War are honored at the National Mall's Vietnam Veterans Memorial.

The Vietnam War was expensive. It killed thousands of US soldiers. Many Americans thought the cause was not worth this loss. They also thought the US military fought too aggressively. They organized anti-war protests.

On October 21, 1967, one of the biggest Vietnam War marches began in Washington, DC. Approximately

100,000 protesters gathered at the Lincoln Memorial. They demanded that US troops leave Vietnam. Faced with this opposition, President Richard Nixon finally ordered the withdrawal of US forces from Vietnam in 1973.

People also protested issues that were happening in the United States. On April 22, 1970, 20 million Americans rallied across the country. They voiced

THE HOLOCAUST MEMORIAL MUSEUM

The United States Holocaust Memorial Museum (USHMM) opened on the National Mall in 1993. It remembers the people who died in the Holocaust. The Holocaust was the mass murder of Jewish people and other persecuted groups during World War II. Germany's Nazi Party committed these murders. Adolf Hitler led the Nazi Party. The Nazis murdered more than 6 million people. Jewish architect James Ingo Freed designed the USHMM. Freed and his family escaped Nazi Germany when he was eight years old. The museum contains artifacts, photographs, and film from Holocaust victims and survivors.

their concerns about pollution and other environmental issues. Some of these people gathered near the Washington Monument. This was the first Earth Day. From then on, Earth Day became an annual holiday. Earth Day raises awareness of environmental issues.

ADDITIONS TO THE NATIONAL MALL

In the 1980s and 1990s, new memorials were built to honor past wars and war veterans. The Vietnam Veterans Memorial was built in 1982. It is made up of two long black walls. The walls are engraved with the names of the nearly 58,000 men and women who died or went missing during the Vietnam War. In 1993, the Vietnam Women's Memorial was built. It is a statue. It depicts two women caring for a US soldier. It honors the contributions of women during the Vietnam War.

In 1995, the Korean War Veterans Memorial was built. It honors the 1.8 million Americans who served in the Korean War (1950–1953). It features a memorial wall and statues of US soldiers.

The Korean War Veterans Memorial includes 19 steel statues of US soldiers who fought in the Korean War.

The National Mall's oldest memorials and monuments were designed in a classical style. This style often featured Greek- or Roman-style columns. Newer memorials and monuments have more modern designs. At first, some people found these designs startling. For example, the Vietnam Veterans Memorial has a simple design. Maya Lin created this design. Lin was a college student studying architecture at the time. Her idea for black memorial walls initially caused controversy. Many people expected the memorial to be grander. But today many visitors consider it to be one of the most moving memorials on the National Mall.

As more memorials were added to the National Mall, some people worried that it was becoming overcrowded. In response, Congress declared that the National Mall was complete in 2003. But many organizations

PERSPECTIVES
MAYA LIN

Maya Lin was 21 years old when she designed the Vietnam Veterans Memorial. She was a student at Yale University. She submitted her design in a national competition. She beat 1,400 other people. Lin wanted to create a memorial that was modern but symbolic. The memorial is made up of two black granite walls. The walls form a V. Lin said this symbolizes a "wound that is closed and healing." She explained, "I wanted something that would just simply say 'They can never come back. They should be remembered.'"

continued to propose new memorials. The World War II Memorial opened in 2004. It honors the 16 million Americans who served in World War II (1939–1945).

Another addition was made to the National Mall in 2004. In that year, the National Museum of the American Indian opened. It contains the country's largest collection of Native American artifacts.

FURTHER EVIDENCE

Chapter Four discusses some of the memorials and monuments that were added to the National Mall from the 1970s to the early 2000s. What was one of the main points of this chapter? What key evidence supports this point? Read the article at the website below. Does the information on the website support this point? Or does it present new evidence?

MONUMENTS AND MEMORIALS

abdocorelibrary.com/national-mall

LOOKING AHEAD

The National Mall has undergone many changes since L'Enfant first designed it more than 200 years ago. On August 23, 2011, some structures on the National Mall were damaged in an earthquake. This included the Washington Monument. Improvements have since been made to the National Mall. But more costly repairs are still needed.

LATEST ADDITIONS

In August 2011, a memorial to civil rights activist Martin Luther King Jr. was unveiled. The memorial is a 30-foot (9-m) statue carved from granite. Behind the statue is a curved wall. Lines from some of King's speeches are carved

Each spring, more than 1.5 million people visit the National Mall to see the cherry trees in bloom.

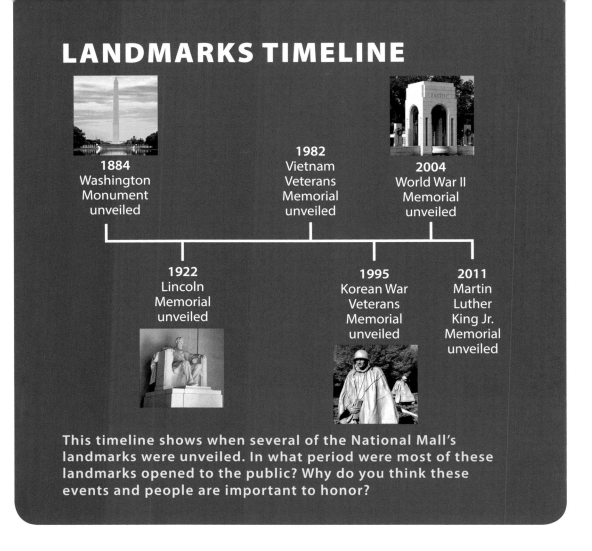

LANDMARKS TIMELINE

1884
Washington Monument unveiled

1922
Lincoln Memorial unveiled

1982
Vietnam Veterans Memorial unveiled

1995
Korean War Veterans Memorial unveiled

2004
World War II Memorial unveiled

2011
Martin Luther King Jr. Memorial unveiled

This timeline shows when several of the National Mall's landmarks were unveiled. In what period were most of these landmarks opened to the public? Why do you think these events and people are important to honor?

on the wall. On the site are 182 cherry blossom trees. The trees reach their full pink bloom each year in April. King was killed on April 4, 1968.

Another recent addition is the Smithsonian National Museum of African American History and Culture (NMAAHC). It opened in 2016. The museum has approximately 36,000 artifacts. The galleries explore African American history from the period of slavery to the present.

AN ENDURING LEGACY

The National Mall offers visitors a look into the country's past. It also sets the stage for the country's future. It continues to be a place where people come to celebrate, protest, and be heard. On January 21, 2017, people around the world participated in the Women's March. They protested for women's rights. More than 100,000 protesters marched in Washington, DC.

PERSPECTIVES

PRESIDENT BARACK OBAMA

On September 24, 2016, President Barack Obama spoke at the opening of the NMAAHC. Thousands of people gathered outside the museum to hear him speak. Obama said the museum "reaffirms that all of us are America—that African American history is not somehow separate from our larger American story, it's not the underside of the American story, it is central to the American story."

CHERRY TREES

The springtime blooming of the cherry trees in Washington, DC, is a popular time of year. Cherry trees were first planted in the city in 1912. In that year, the mayor of Tokyo, Japan, sent 3,000 trees to the capital as a gift. The city's cherry trees attract many visitors. Each year, people visit the capital during the National Cherry Blossom Festival. This festival lasts three weeks. It features parades, kite festivals, and Japanese lantern lighting.

Today, the National Mall has many features and attractions. There are also areas for sports and recreation, such as volleyball courts. The National Mall contains 26 miles (42 km) of sidewalks and 8 miles (13 km) of bike trails.

The National Mall will likely change in the future to reflect more of the people and events that have shaped US history. Organizations continue to advocate for new additions. The National Mall may look different in the future. But it will endure as a symbol of democracy and national identity.

STRAIGHT TO THE
SOURCE

Lonnie Bunch is the founding director of the NMAAHC. In an interview, he spoke about the building's design. He said:

> *The Mall is America's front yard, but it is also, in some ways, the place where more people come to understand what it means to be an American than anyplace else in the country. I wanted a darker building. I didn't want the white marble building that traditionally was [on] the Mall. What I wanted to say was, there's always been a dark presence in America that people undervalue, neglect, overlook. I wanted this building to say that. I also wanted a building that spoke of resiliency and uplift.*

Source: Vinson Cunningham. "Making a Home for Black History." *The New Yorker*. The New Yorker, August 22, 2016. Web. Accessed May 24, 2019.

Back It Up

The author of this passage is using evidence to support a point. Write a paragraph describing the point the author is making. Then write down two or three pieces of evidence the author uses to make the point.

IMPORTANT
DATES

1790
President George Washington signs the Residence Act. This act allows him to choose a site for a permanent capital city. He chooses a site in Maryland and Virginia along the Potomac and Anacostia Rivers. This site later becomes known as Washington, DC.

1848
Construction of the Washington Monument begins. The monument is completed in 1885.

1861
The American Civil War breaks out. The City of Washington becomes the headquarters for the Union army.

1902
The McMillan Plan is created. Improvements and updates are made to the capital city.

August 28, 1963
Activists march on the National Mall to bring attention to civil rights issues. This protest is called the March on Washington for Jobs and Freedom.

1982
The Vietnam Veterans Memorial opens.

2004
The World War II Memorial opens.

2016
The Smithsonian National Museum of African American History and Culture opens.

STOP AND
THINK

Tell the Tale

Chapter One of this book explores one person's experience at the National Mall. Imagine you and your family are taking a trip to the National Mall. Write 200 words about the sites you want to see. Why are these sites important? Why do you want to visit them?

Surprise Me

Chapter Two describes the early history of Washington, DC, and the formation of the National Mall. After reading this book, what two or three facts about the National Mall's early history surprised you? Write a few sentences about each fact. Why did you find each fact surprising?

Take a Stand

Some people think the National Mall is becoming overcrowded. Others think more memorials should be added. Do you think the National Mall should be expanded or changed? Why or why not? How do you think the National Mall would change if more memorials were added?

You Are There

This book discusses how the US capital was designed and developed. Imagine you are living in the capital city in the mid-1800s. Write a letter home telling your friends how the city has changed over the years. What do you think is the most important change that people should know about? Be sure to add plenty of details to your letter.

GLOSSARY

advocate
to publicly support a cause

allied
partnered with

Communist
relating to Communism, a political system in which all people in a society share their goods with each other

discrimination
the unjust treatment of a person or group based on race or other perceived differences

memorial
something that honors an important person or event

monument
a type of memorial that is often a building or statue

obelisk
a tall pillar with a top shaped like a pyramid

secede
to officially separate from something

segregation
the separation of people of different races or ethnic groups through separate schools and other public spaces

simulator
a machine that shows people what it is like to operate a vehicle or an aircraft

veteran
someone who has served in the military

ONLINE RESOURCES

To learn more about the National Mall, visit our free resource websites below.

Visit **abdocorelibrary.com** or scan this QR code for free Common Core resources for teachers and students, including vetted activities, multimedia, and booklinks, for deeper subject comprehension.

Visit **abdobooklinks.com** or scan this QR code for free additional online weblinks for further learning. These links are routinely monitored and updated to provide the most current information available.

LEARN MORE

Harris, Duchess. *The March on Washington and Its Legacy*. Minneapolis, MN: Abdo Publishing, 2019.

Rodgers, Kelly. *Our Nation's Capital*. Huntington Beach, CA: Teacher Created Materials, 2015.

INDEX

About the Author

Jamie Kallio is a librarian in the south suburbs of Chicago. She is the author of many nonfiction books for children. Her favorite subjects to learn about are history and cats.